JACK MAPANJE was born in Kadango Village, Malawi in 1944 and has lived in Malawi and in Britain. His first collection, *Of Chameleons and Gods*, was published by Heinemann in 1981 and in 1988, it received the Rotterdam International Poetry Award. Mapanje has also co-edited *Oral Poetry From Africa: an Anthology* with Landeg White (Longman, 1983) and *Summer Fires: an Anthology of Modern African Poetry* with Cosmo Piertese and Angus Calder (Heinemann, 1983).

On its second reprint, *Of Chameleons and Gods* was banned in Malawi and Mapanje was subsequently detained in Mikuyu Maximum Detention Centre near Zomba for three years, seven months and sixteen days. No charges were brought against him. He was released in May 1991 following intense pressure from fellow writers and activists. At present he lives in England with his wife and three children.

'. . . full of fine physical imagery, acute observation and a strong sense of his own roots and values . . . Mapanje is fresh, lively and aggressively inventive.' *London Magazine*

JACK MAPANJE

THE CHATTERING WAGTAILS OF MIKUYU PRISON

HEINEMANN

Heinemann Educational Publishers
Halley Court, Jordan Hill, Oxford OX2 8EJ
A Division of Reed Educational & Professional Publishing Ltd

Heinemann: A Division of Reed Publishing (USA) Inc.
361 Hanover Street, Portsmouth, NH 03801-3912, USA

Heinemann Educational Books (Nigeria) Ltd
PMB 5205, Ibadan

Heinemann Educational Botswana (Publishers) (Pty) Ltd
PO Box 10103, Village Post Office, Gaborone, Botswana

MELBOURNE   AUCKLAND
FLORENCE   PRAGUE   MADRID   ATHENS
SINGAPORE   TOKYO   SAO PAULO
CHICAGO   PORTSMOUTH (NH)   MEXICO CITY
IBADAN   GABORONE   JOHANNESBURG
KAMPALA   NAIROBI

First published by Heinemann International Literature and Textbooks
in 1993

ISBN 0 435 91198 8

Series Editors:
Chinua Achebe 1962–1990
Adewale Maja-Pearce 1990–94

Series Consultant: Abdulrazak Gurnah 1994–97

Phototypeset by
Wilmaset Ltd, Birkenhead, Wirral
Printed and bound in Great Britain by
Cox & Wyman Ltd, Reading, Berkshire

97   98   99   10   9   8   7   6   5   4   3   2

To the memory of my mother, Victoria
Mereresi Ziyabu, who gave up waiting
(to give us room to move) and died
two months before I was released from
Mikuyu Prison.

And for the love and resilience
of Mercy, Judith, Lunda and Lika
and the good humour of the inmates
at Mikuyu Prison, Zomba, Malawi.

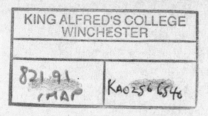

*'Spare me the din of your chanting,
let me hear none of your strumming on lyres,*

*but let justice flow like water
and uprightness like a never-failing stream!'*

AMOS 5: 24–5

*'When a ruler listens to false reports,
all his ministers will be scoundrels.'*

PROVERBS 29: 12

Acknowledgements

Acknowledgements are due to the editors of the following publications in which some of these poems first appeared: *London Magazine, Stand Magazine, Poetry Wales, Index on Censorship, Kunapipi, Saiwa, Rotterdam Poetry International, Malawi Writers Group, The Kenyon Review, The Loft, Oxford Magazine, Prison Writing, The Page, The Kalahari Review, Tees Valley Writer* and the authors of *The Twitter Machine* (Basil Blackwell, 1989), *Curing Their Ills* (Stanford University Press, 1991), and *Power and the Praise Poem* (University Press of Virginia, 1991).

And grateful thanks to the Poetry Society and the Irina Trust, London; Society for the Protection of Science and Learning, London; Fund for Free Expression, New York; Poetry International Award, Rotterdam; International PEN throughout the world; linguists and writers in Africa, the UK, America and other parts of the world; Amnesty International; Africa Watch; students, churchmen, friends and colleagues all over the freedom-loving world; for their fight for my freedom and for their assistance which enabled my family and me to travel to the UK and stay at the University of York in 1991–2 where this volume was assembled. The final version was completed with the generous support of St Antony's and Exeter Colleges, Oxford, as well as the Northern, Yorkshire and Humberside, and North West Arts Boards who offered me a research fellowship and Greater North International Writer's Residency respectively in 1992–3.

Contents

Prologue

From the vault of Chingwe's Hole
Come these chattering wagtails,

Desperate voices of fractured souls
Nesting on desert walls of prisons

And exiles, afflicted or self-imposed,
Counting stubborn beads, deprived

Laughters and ceaseless tears shed
In the chaos of invented autocracies

Now darkly out of bounds beyond
These tranquil walls of York.

Justice!

JACK MAPANJE, HEWORTH, FEBRUARY 1993

ANOTHER FOOLS' DAY
HOMES IN

Another Fools' Day Touches Down: Shush

(For Mercy, Judith, Lunda & Lika, 1983)

Another Fools' Day touches down, another homecoming . . .
Shush. Bunting! some anniversary; they'll be preoccupied;
Only a wife, children and a friend, probably waiting.

A PhD, three books, a baby-boy, three and half years –
Some feat to put us . . . Shush. Such frivolities no longer
Touch people here. 'So, you decided to come back, eh?'

Rhetorical questions dredge up spastic images . . . Shush.
In the dusty, brown-grey landscape, the heat unrolls.
Some wizard has locked up his rainbows and thunder again!

Why do the gods hold up the rains? Don't we praise them enough?
Shush. There are no towers here, no domes or gothic windows.
Only your children, friends, nestling up for a warm story.

Kadango Village, Even Milimbo Lagoon Is Dry

(For Landeg & Alice, 1983)

In the cracking heat of October, our village market.
A queue of skeletal hands reaching out for the last
Cowlac tin of loose grain, falters, against hope.

In the drought, a frail dog sniffing his lover's arse
Goes berserk, barking at the wave of grey eddying
Between the mountain boulders and the shrivelling lake.

Scurvy children kicking the grit, scud beachwards,
Their wobbly feet digging in for possible cassava
Where even such tubers are now hushed in shoot.

Rocky geckos, blue tongues hanging out, scuttle on
The hot sand but bil-tong, belly-up, before the beach.
Fish eagles suspended, swoop down for grasshoppers.

Even Milimbo lagoon is dead; no oar dips in any more.
Those fishermen who dreamt up better weather
Once, no longer cast their nets here, and their

Delightful bawdy songs to bait the droughts are
Cloaked in the choking fumes of dawn, banned. But
Our fat-necked custodians despatch another tale.

Of Our Chiefs and Their Concubines

Last Christmas, they sat beside the hearths
Secure, together, cracking roast chestnuts

Or stale jokes about hollies and ivies
As red wines cooled down another hot year

Today, even the vines threaten to stream
The streets with banners of another fire.

Easter Apologies for Bubble Dreams

You dreamt of a room of your own,
With mother's ostrich-neck clay jars
(Decked in mystic beads and triangles)
Shaping the four corners and lianas
From them straying up the ceiling;

You hoped for the delicate carves
Of village ladles and wood masks and
Home gourds the children would paint
In Easter-egg colours, pendulous on
Your light-blue walls. Outside, you

Saw the jasmine sweetening the pears,
The peaches and the tender palm trees;
So that if I needed metaphors, you
Teased, I shouldn't have to patrol
The woods of Chingwe's Hole, shame-

lessly startling the squirrels on heat
Or the sparrows ministering to the rock-
owls snoring to the gentle splashes of
Mulungusi river; and if the children
Should want branches for Palm Sunday,

They'd merely run the backyard boughs
As we munched our pawpaw sandwiches.
But it was not to be, dear, and if our joys
Had chanced by your dream, we'd probably
Have aggravated the children's asthma!

The Haggling Old Woman at Balaka

The old woman at Balaka never stops
She haggles over every new event:

'I was fed on breasts and goat milk,
Not on your silly, dust-milk-tins!
And you girls today are cocked up,
You sell chicken eggs for cokes and fantas
To suckle your babies, then you ask me
Why your babies are rickets and ribs?

Now you come to lend me money, you say,
To buy fertilizers to improve my yield.
How generous, how degrading! And I must
Suppose your banks won't dry out! Can't
You see I am too tired for these tricks?

And from now on I will keep my crop to
Myself – you have no shame building your
Brick houses on old women's dying energies
Under the lie of national development!
No, I've sung too many tattered praises,
Spare me these spotted desires, children . . .'

Dear granny at Balaka fidgets too much,
I fear what she'll brag about next.

The Rise of the New Toadies (1983)

(For Felix Mnthali)

The streaming blood of luscious Zomba strawberries
Coagulates today. A cold spell overcasts this plateau

No cheeky lads hop about with granadilla bastketfuls.
No black Mercedes slithers about the compounds below.

Road blocks. The silent megaphones blurt, 'Any more
Yobbos try their liberal jokes again, gun-point burial.

No undertakers. We police your keyholes, jam your foreign
Radios. No bishop fidgets about requiem masses: church-gates

Char. Otherwise, village exit visas for "rebel" presbyters.
The self-imposed curfew starts at seven. Beyond that

Everybody sniffs from the backyard of their fuming huts,
To spare the people further slanderous outside lies . . .'

Apparently, the 'yobbos' only wanted the air cleared, but
The other toadies wouldn't wait; you know the pattern!

For Another Village Politburo Projected

Today, those bloated icons and brazen hacks will
Convene again: squirrels in kinked flywhisks,
Flashing their nausea, will marvel at the cedar
Walls of this great hall gurgling their eulogies;
Hyenas with the gilt of our skulls behind will
Tumble in chicken bones fattened by the meagre
Women of this village; brusque bumble-bees glutted
Will woo their dung-beetles – who will not show up
Here? We will all tune in to these levities, some
Plodding on to the dais, others shrugging without
Bitterness. And like yesterday, we will forge no new
Vision, but nuzzling Adam and Queen Bee, we'll baa
The same anthem: when did our swastika ever starve?
(Unless some soldier-bee cracks in on us one day!)

No, Creon, There's No Virtue in Howling

'It is no glory to kill and kill again.'
Teiresias, *Antigone*.

No, Creon, you overstate your image to your
People. No, there's no virtue in howling so.
How can you hope to repair Haemon, your
Own blood, our only hope for the throne,
By reproaching his body mangled by your
Decree and put to rest without the requiem
Of our master drums? What tangential sentries
Advise you to bemoan the dead by scoffing
Them publicly thus? Those accidents your
Flunkies master-stroked, those tortures &
Exiles fashioned, and the blood you loved
To hear, did we need more lies? Look now,
Even the village lads toss their coins for old
Creon's days. What cowardice, what perversity
Grates life-laden minds on our death-beds?

The 1984 Martyrs' Day Prayer

If this is how you'd have us pray to you, O Lord,
With this last egg from a matted bird startled
This scruffy coin from a street beggar beaten
This lean goat from flummoxed chaperons plucked

This sacrificial lamb from the shrines usurped
Our Chief's bull down their banquet halls flashed
Their abandoned adulteresses upon us 'rebels' set
This arena of schemers, scratching their boils in

Public, for another grave, unnecessary assault –
If this be how you'd have us praise you, O Lord,
Be gentle to this mortal, whose crime was only
The tipple on Martyrs' Day: break this neck nobly.

When the Shire Valley Dries Up Patiently

(For Megan Vaughan)

The crime is how we deliberately keep out of touch,
Pretending it has nothing to do with us, we've been
Through it all. Baobab fruit & grilled mice on clay plate,
How familiar the metaphors, we think, suspecting our
House servants of having killed & eaten our pet cats!
We do not feel the green mangoes drying up in the sun
Outside or the lorries festering in the backyards. And
When the naked women crowded at the village borehole
Begin knocking pails of water off each other's heads,
We wonder what the fight is about, those funny drunks!
At the University, expatriate lecturers gesticulate,
Finger the leaves of Marx to a batch of yawning students,
Nervously trying to define something or other, their
Wives cheerfully wiping their bums on local News
After *nsima* dishes! Going local gently, they cautiously
Chide. But like the jacarandas we blossom indifferently
As our governors gravely worry about: 'These free
Japanese TV offers, Honourable Minister, should we
Really introduce them into the villages now, do you think?'
Colonies of storks in flamboyant trees look down on
The valley dust and the last of the sweet bananas.

Vigil for a Fellow Credulous Captive

(For Anenenji)

Someday perhaps he too will come back home,
Not like a lion avenging his muzzle once shattered
Nor a cheetah stalking his long awaited prey.
No dead bones, however tough, ever take on flesh
Again, outside myths. No, someday Anenenji will
Surface as bones, mere bones, brittly washed up this
Makokola beach, scattered by the morning breakers
Of this gentle lake. And the rough sack they shoved
Him in will drift along in shreds, perhaps hanging
Delicately to a yellowing drove of waterlilies or
Some sudd, forgotten; the heavy millstone once on his
Legs having broken free. Only then will it probably
Dawn on us to cast our mask and gather those frosty
Mornings he spent picking tea for a weekly handful
Of cheerless, foggy tickies; those blistering afternoons
He clambered up distant craggy hills to sell Party Cards
– A credulous captive to some dreamer's dementia!
From door to door coercing, like one venting his displaced
Rut; sometimes thrice in season, insisting every baby
Bought a Party Card: for the market, the bus, life . . .
What moved him, what his wife saw, you could not guess.
Not even once when you, feverishly bemused by all this
Fuss of only a mortal against other mortals, tracked
The splintered bare-feet chugging homeward with a full
Purse to the area Party Headquarters or watched those
Cracked hands rolling coils of brown tobacco, puffing
And rescuing by the tail a maimed lizard dropped from
The cobweb bamboo rafters; not after sharing his pop maize
For dinner even, could you tell what he really cared for
And why. But today a mute wife before a crushed paraffin

Tincan lamp keeps vigil over Anenenji's fireplace; alone.
Nobody, no mound or tombstone stands to say where
Or what justice he might have suffered. Perhaps someday
He'll come again with another pack of Cards to sell,
   menacing!

Anenenjis: eminent public figures whose only crime is to believe in non-corrupt, just and free society.

OUT OF BOUNDS

Seasoned Jacarandas

(For Frank Chipasula)

Stiff collared, hands in pockets,
spitting out phlegm and scanning
the point of thankless patriotic
wakes and timid nights, we lied
brother, believing we would soon
arrive, someone must hang around,
knowing there would be no pieces
(the true warmth was outside). Today,
though seasoned, our metaphors
blanch. The jacarandas still deeply
purple our pavements; but for once
their pop under foot or tyre chills,
like those still fresh squads firing.
Who'll watch whose wake tomorrow,
this self-imposed siege trembles!

Smiller's Bar Revisited (1983)

No, how do you know they no longer seek what
Their hearts desire those girls at Smiller's Bar?

Note how they sneer at your dawns & bonfires now
That you have accidentalized their beloved

Combatants. And having known so many nebulous
Fleas, why shouldn't they claim vague memories

Of your so-called liberation struggle? And in this
Feminist age, grant them revised metaphors, man!

You can't be so sure your buttercups gather here
Only to scent down the few rebels their masters

(Mindless-brittle-neck-hackers!) still invent
For them and what nonsense, what paranoia!

It's true at counters the masters lurch to your
Side, offering you round after round of beer,

Setting up their abandoned adulteresses for you
To settle on and enjoying their sadistic stories:

'That rhinoceros you gunned down scratching
His livid wounds on pepperwood, wasn't it fun

How he collapsed, twitching', they laugh hoping
You can join in the joke & be properly convicted!

But you must concede, after you accidentalized
Their Anenenjis, the nuance of your classical

Butterfly today slips away & even you don't know
Who the real master is when, from her creased

Victorian frock, she rectifies your change without
Blush & pontificates about inflation having

Trebled her price. Indeed why should anybody's
Bastard at home eat grass? So, give the girls

A break, let the coloured bulbs, drunken moths
& robot drums choke the bay; who said freedom's

Not a bifurcated pig? Revisiting Smiller's Bar
May be the beginning of your true liberation!

accidentalize: to kill and pretend it was an accident when everybody knows it
was not (first used by the Writers Group, Chancellor College, University of
Malawi, 1983/4).

21

Baobab Fruit Picking (or Development in Monkey Bay)

(For Mary & David Kerr)

'We've fought before, but this is worse than rape!'
In the semi-Sahara October haze, the raw jokes

Of Balamanja women are remarkable. The vision
We revel in has sent their husbands to the mines

Of Jo'burg, to buy us large farms, she insists.
But here, the wives survive by their wits & sweat:

Shoving dead cassava stalks into rocks, catching
Fish in tired *chitenje* cloths with kids, picking

Baobab fruit & whoring. The bark from the baobab
They strip into strings for their reed wattle,

The fruit they crack, scoop out the white, mix with
Goat milk, 'That's porridge for today, children!'

The shell is drinking gourd or firewood split
(They used to grate the hard cores into girls'

Initiation oil once). 'But you imported the Boers,
Who visited our Chief at dawn, promising boreholes!'

These pine cottages on the beach shot up instead, some
With barbed wire fences fifty yards into the lake!

(What cheek!) Now each weekend, the 'blighted-tomato-
thighs in reeking loin-cloths' come, boating, grinning

At them baobab fruit picking. 'My house was right
Here!' Whoever dares check these Balamanja dreamers?

Moving into Monkey Bay (Balamanja North)

After their pine beach cottages
Moving into Balamanja North blunders

No monkey beckons to you under
The dappled shade of palm-trees

No one hacks the occasion free with
Phangas. Balamanja North is bush

Still to be priced; only sandwiches
& beer grace the take-over bid.

A canoe. Timorous hands after years
Without oars. In the gloaming breeze,

The bay drifts with blue-knotted
Waterlilies. Brown leaves rotting

& decayed baobab fruit entangle in
The sudd contrasting the live shells

On the shore. But how do bull-frogs
Come to grief amongst dragonflies here?

The canoe cannot pass. The oar's dip
Releases a throng of anopheles. Note,

We have company: after belching with
Sacks of charcoal & finding steel bolts

The gates to his prospective buyer,
After trudging back to his tin-roof

Hovel & perhaps a brisk quarrel with his
Wife, who should picnic his desires on

My bay? I shoo the mosquitoes & row in.

The Farms That Gobble the Land at Home*

The farms peacefully chew up the land at home
Bulldozing docile mudhuts, flattening broken
Reed shacks into neatly developed cakes, scatter-
ing their goats, chickens, pigeons or mice in
The swirling sand which blinds the eyes at home.
One farmer gathers smaller farmers into WETs
(Wage-Earning-Tenants) offering them thirty coins
Per day, stopping their mixed planting: cheap
Original ashes or compost manures are banned
(To maximize profits) and fertilizers (only farms
Can afford) imposed. Men no longer need the mines
For gold; even women become breadwinners (with
Specially planned female wages to ensure their
Domestic sweat is not impaired) on the land our
Fathers fought for us back home. Moonlight drums,
Fireside yarns are ripped under the auspices of
Rural Growth Centres & recreations (such as
Whoring) carefully instituted to breed foreign
Exchange (for our guns, droughts or videos). But
When it rains (kindly), the snails still drag
Along their shells, the frogs hop about their
Monotonous stalls; only they mustn't croak about
Their daily dregs or the pesticides which blacken
Their skins & corrode their lungs, lest huge blue
Or green caterpillars on patrol crush them. So, when
You walk about, only Peace & Calm Law & Order
Prevails on the fields that gobble the land at home.

*After Kofi Awoonor, Ghana.

Flying Over the Summer Haze of Home (1983/4)

Why is our African summer so unsettling?
Why must flying over home sink the heart?

In Rwanda we joked about their proto-banana
Beer but their dense proto-drought was not

Amusing, hanging thus like industrial dust
On faceless banana fronds whittling them.

Swaziland smogs Queen of Sheba's breasts
Reducing eminent witch-doctors into trackers

Of prostitute ghosts beside Mbabane cliffs
After their devastating cyclones. Outside

Harare, Domboshawa crickets shriek in dry
Monotones. And the fierce lions of Nairobi,

Lean from the heat of National Park, road-
block the airport highway to bemused tourist

Shutters. Even from these heights of Ku Chawe
Inn of Zomba plateau no army tanks lumber in

Or out of Chingwe's Hole below; no visiting
Seasoned German pilot dares hang-glide his way

Down this tough brown tissue as onerous army-
worms nibble at the last of the green leaves.

We bored our way through nameless thickets
Of cloud above hoping for the rains below

But secretly fearing we'd merely sit and note
Stinking dung-beetles pushing their lot into

Chingwe's Hole (with no charm to foretell our
Rains in this world without a horizon). And

When does this haze intend to lift? Sometimes
It feels like you are watching mountain fires

Just contained or a huge down-pour of December
Rains is at hand or finally here! But no, it's

Another October, arid and hot; and somewhere
In that ubiquitous haze another babe will drop.

Burning the Witch for Rains (The Dark Case)

(For Pat O'Malley)

Is this perhaps the last of our dear old sluts
This witch frowning vacantly, condemned only

By her snuff-black gums & the stark veins?
When did matriarchal bones living in rotten

Thatch hatchback become a menace, people?
& does she muse upon her grimy shroud or

The bane of our brittle existence? Malignant
Village vigilantes stack up dry acacia twigs

& brambles, smarting for the witch's fire
After our cheek flaying, head shaving ritual.

The stern, omnipotent hand uncovers official
Evidence: exhibit one, an amorphous dark case

She's supposed to have locked up lightning
& thunder so the rains don't come. When one

Zealot opened it at the police station, the box's
Bowels growled like bloodhounds, blinding him.

(The curious jury of kids bends with laughter.)
Exhibit two, the bag of fertilizer she stole.

The malcontent apparently still believes in her
Mixed-planting with ashes & compost manures;

Dare the rebellious dreadlocks resist as barking
Youth-leaguers dive for their bloody antic rites . . . ?

For Fear of Which Mandrax Images & Which Death?

Clouds of adversity are gathering on mountain
Tops. Last Saturday, guerrillas overran Kaporo

Lynching three constables; but the local MP's
Newsclip stresses, 'It was only bandits & you

Still love me, anyway!' The radio cracks with
More callous trivia shamelessly inventing new

Rebels for the gallows. When head-shaven hang-
man, vigilante-flanked, swoops in for his rites,

Nerves rack; where & how did this village seize
Its chronic malaria that even quinine flowing

Into its veins by drip won't do? What miasma
Brought this cancerous growth that nobody wants

To broach for fear of death? We all know their
Bogus faces in the corridors, but when we pass

The Mandrax images, we merely chuckle at the in-
ward truths we know we share but won't admit

For fear of dubbing each other liars. Even our
Snoop's metaphors are anaemic & scatty. The poor

Cockroach must be wondering now whether it was
Worth it, hiding those lonely tears of Chingale

Mother whose child was bellowed to death by breath
Of god's helicopter on earth. If the children

Still rudely ask about that lorry the women high-
jacked to their Party meeting, 'Whatever became

Of the protesting driver, as metal, woman & rock
Mangled down canyon?' If children wonder about

The Bibles & Eggs offered at a tars every bumper
Rains, 'When do they multiply?' What of us? What

Incurable despair has gripped us that our lips
Won't open? For fear of which elusive death?

Chilling Jan Smuts Airport In-Transito (1984)

(For Lupenga Mphande)

I never thought I would reach this patch
Of carved Europe, landing thus cautiously;

I never imagined the musty air of this sudden
Limbo. How does one avoid racist metaphors

Where white dominates the shuffling morning
Queues ordering you into passport slots?

(My Tanzanian colleague insists no Boer stamp
In his passport!) Even those multiracial Air

Zimbabwe girls, charming in their confident
Shona, Ndebele and English a flight ago must

Mill around uneasy in the chill of Jan Smuts.
Elsewhere noisy kids would be sliding down

Those lovely escalators or running up and
Down trying to beat them; but here only giddy

White soldiers crowd the escalators though
No ANC threatens to molotov Jan Smuts Airport.

At the inquiry desk, the white woman in pink-
stuck smile immediately confirms the stand-by

Tickets from our white American acquaintances
With boarding passes best wishes to Manzini

And free access to Johannesburg delights but
She tosses us brown in-transito cards to get

Us into the lounge and buy us things though
The duty-free shop demands boarding passes before

Transaction: confessing our six hour stand-by
Also to Manzini, their transparent doors lock.

Our embarrassed Americans argue for our rights
But Jan Smuts' winking cues disarm such liberal

Efforts. And since your travellers' cheques are
Kindly cashed for you behind drawn bars, why don't

You join the other passengers in the lounge bar
Sipping beer, tea or coffee with chins-in-palms?

Watch that Zimbabwean white radical who's been
Through this before. She has been visiting her

Daughter married in Cape Town and now pours out
Her heart: 'When we reached this stage, sleeping

With guns under our pillows, we knew it was all
Over; but they do not understand in Cape Town

And I give them ten years!' she bets generously
As fuddled, gasping glottals, cracking through

The microphones, marshal passengers to gate five;
She rises like a shebeen ghost staggering home.

Is it prudent to phone up Jaki at Skotaville?
I rake up Ingoapele's recent arrest in Soweto.

On Banning Of Chameleons and Gods
(June, 1985)

The fragrance of your banning order is not
Pungent enough after four years & one re-
print dear sister & your brother's threat,
'Your chameleons poke at the raw wounds of
Our nation!' won't rhyme however much you
Try. To ban, burn or to merely withdraw from
Public engagement, what's the difference? It
Still humiliates our readers, you & me. And
What do you see in these senile chameleons,
These gouty, mythical gods & libertine Mphunzi
Leopards to warrant all the heat? Haven't you
Heard the children's riddles yet or the jokes
At the market place about your chiefs & their
Concubines? How do you enjoy squinting only
At lines without bothering to ask what even
Swallows perched on the barbed wires of your
Central Prisons already know? Who does not
Know who pokes at whose nation's wounds raw?
& why should my poking at wounds matter more
Than your hacking at people's innocent necks?
No, for children's sake, unchain these truths;
Release the verse you've locked in our hearts!

April Wishes for 20 Gordon Square, London
(A Letter, 1987)

I

Dear Neil, as the toxic lizards of home crowd
In on us today, I recall those barriers in
Linguistics Gordon Square is so good at knocking
Down. You know how little I cared about those
Concrete gates that suspected me mugger on High
Street Barnet or framed in those hypocritical
Digs of Balham whether I sang about Wimbledon
Strawberries & cream or not. And knowing what
We know about dawns and bonfires, I believe I
Was not meant to map out Africa's dawn from
The dark alleys of London & I make no apology
For being a late visionary. It was kind I was
Spared the Victorian euphoria of bowler hats,
Flywhisks and image-fracturing London blitzes
That my fusty ancestors forever drill down our
Throats & flaked by those smoking tongues of
Brixton & Wood Green, it would have been dis-
honest to have pretended otherwise. So, here's
The season's peace for the crowd at the square.

II

And dear Harun-Al Rashid, as the scorpions
Of Zomba gather at our keyholes to hear what
They have sewn, the kola nuts you offered me
Now sharpen. Jolting in that rusty, chattering
Citroën from the steel benches of Gordon Square
To the mouldy walls of York, I forgot to ask
Where you got kola nuts to break in the heart
Of London & the gates of York? And today, I
Discovered those photographs you forced on me

Boasting the York Linguistics Conference (with
Me sampling Stones and floating to inscrutable
Punk & you salaaming Mecca by the hour & steering
My 'rough' ways, you said). I hope you understand
Though: on my edge of Africa, without Opec Oil
Or golden stools to show off about, kola nuts
Were merely symbolic fetters, bitter, crumbly,
Not like spearmint gum & photographs cold.
But as the Shepherd's Bush offals we shared &
The *Daily Mirror* cones we ate our chips from
Come back today, I thought you might like to
Look at these bristly negatives, with love?

Out of Bounds (or Our Maternity Asylum)

I was out of bounds, they insisted, outside
The wards, where iron roofs crumble under

Rotting *mlombwa* leaves, green paint rusts
To two decades of dead dust, windows are

Covered in shreds of matting (to stop our
Scorpion pneumonia of June?). Inside, some

Sixty inmates of spasming women top & tail
On thirty beds; ninety others with infants

Scramble over the cracked cold cement floor –
A family under each bed, most in between.

A fresh smelling babe in the corner grinds.
Mother suckles him gnawing at her tatters.

On a slab, a cramped enamel plate (with
A piece of tripe she could not chew) labours.

But this is no asylum & no one is fighting
The desert war here. These are refugees only

From Child Spacing, atoning for the ghost
Revolution twenty years ago, repaired in this

Shrinking hospital God knows how. And I gather
The doctors & nurses who toil twenty-four hours

(With blunt needles, without drugs, on a small
Wage) offered to extend this wing: there was

The usual hiccup about official clearance.
Yet this was the rallying cry of the dais

Once upon a time. And when the powers visit
The sick at Christmas, some caesareans will be

Prematurely discharged: others jostled into
Neat lines, clapping their praises. The windows

Will have been glazed, the blood-bespattered
Walls painted. They'll borrow beds & canvases

From the nearby hospital so Father Christmas
Sees one patient per bed: another dream done!

But I hear, I am out of bounds?

CHATTERING WAGTAILS

The Streak-Tease at Mikuyu Prison,
25 September 1987

(For Alec Pongweni)

It was not like the striptease at the Birds' Nest
On London Street Paddington in the seventies, with

Each piece undone underscored by the thump of
Your pint of London Bitter & your analysis of

The structure of English pub vowels; nor was it
Like that male streaker, in the Three Day Week,

Stark & ugly, running around Talbot Square as we
Chuckled about the pleasures humans can engage in.

The streak-tease at Mikuyu Prison is an affair
More sportive. First, the ceremony of handcuff

Disposal, with the warder's glib remarks about how
Modern handcuffs really dug in when you tried to

Fidget; then the instructions: take off your glasses,
Your sweater, your shirt. Shove these with your

Jacket into their shroud-white bag or your handbag
Until your release, which could be tomorrow, if you

Are lucky, and he seriously means release anyday
(Haven't I heard about the four parliamentarians

Who stayed one night here, then got 'released'
The next day?). The spine chills at this revelation

& the prospect of another mysterious death; and if
Your naked belly should droop & you feel the stench

Of yesterbooze, why blame God for abandoning you in
These walls named after figs? Now the trousers' turn,

Strip by strip, to see the absence of razor-blades,
Pencils & pins (these bring leg-irons & more handcuffs

Here). The pockets must be emptied of all other
Items too; especially, 'the change' from Gymkhana

Club: nobody wants the reputation of stealing
Prisoners' change! And murderers awaiting hanging

At Mikuyu hide *chamba* & things in their anus; so
Do us the honour of bending. And the guards wonder

What pants University balls sit in; take that down
Too; but it's not yet law in Mikuyu to roll your

Banana (the humour is extravagant here). Finally,
The shoes & socks: pleading blisters on that bad

Foot brings another string of ministers & rebels
More distinguished, who have followed these rules.

Dare you fight further after ten hours in cock-
roach custody? Let the shroud-white pocketless

Gown & pocketless shorts (they call them *foya*),
Wrap that shivering midnight body. Their questions

Are late, 'So they took you from Gymkhana Club?'
Or their advice, 'You must be more careful; these

People are out to finish us, you see?' When locks
Give way, 'That Chemistry Professor friend of yours

Was the dullest I knew in Standard Six but now . . .'
Now the stinking shit-bucket tripped over drowns

The news about the lights being left overnight for
You to scare night creepers, as the putrid *bwezi*

Blanket-rag enters the single cell & staggers on to
The cracked cold cement floor of Mikuyu Prison.

Fears from Mikuyu Cells for Our Loves

Our neighbours' nerves behind those
Trimmed pine hedges of Chingwe's Hole
And the strategies they'll adopt when

They are approached by the Special
Branch, are familiar but horrify;
We rehearsed their betrayals weekly:

'Where did you first meet, I mean,
What did he often boast about in bars;
When he played darts, what jokes?

Didn't he, in your considered view,
Behave in a manner prejudicial? So,
He bent even those straight lectures!

Did your children ever mix with his
And how often did your wife share
Home-ground maize flour with his?'

We recycled other fears ad nauseam too
And what tricks to perform to thrive;
Only the victims' hour did we not know.

I recall, when our neighbour was
Taken eleven years ago, secret tears
On my wife's cheeks because visiting

His wife and kids or offering them
Our sweet potatoes in broad day was
A crime, her husband had just been

Invented 'rebel'; on the third day
University Office quickly issued her
Exit visa to her husband's village.

The feasts of our singular friends
We also reran: 'His detention was
Overdue, those poems! Don't mention

That name in my office; I hear he
Refused to apologize, how typical!
How is that woman and her kids still

Occupying that University house?
Those conferences he loved, it's us
Going now. Has he reached Mikuyu then?

We thought it was another joke!'
Today, I see your delicate laughter
And what abuse they'll hurl at you

Dear children, dear mother, my dear
Wife as your 'rebel' dad confronts
The wagtail shit of Mikuyu Prison:

'Shore up their brittle feet, Lord!'

The Chattering Wagtails of Mikuyu Prison

I

Welcome to the chattering wagtails of
D4. Before your Gymkhana Club story,
Let's begin with the history of the wing
You've come from. They call it the New
Building, which is so marvellously blank
As you saw, that you'd have cracked up
Within months, however tough-willed;
Thank these D4s for moving you here.

II

When the Secretary General of the Party
First conceived the New Building it was
On behalf of the people, to liberate
Them from the despot they'd nominated
For life and who had extorted their
Traditional naivety to his craze. And
When the Chief of Special Branch chose
Himself head of detentions and detainees,
The two conspired to cure the monster's
Tics permanently here. So, they built
Those brown brick cells, four in front
And four behind, three paces by two
Each, whitewashing the walls inside,
To remind the tyrant of the bit of
Colour he would soon miss or to give
Him a chance to vent his wise yearning
In the manner of all graffiti. They
Separated the four front cells from
The four back cells with a thin wall
Through which you could shout messages
To each other at the risk of handcuffs

And leg-irons chained to the stocks.
They built a courtyard, sixty-five bricks
High, twelve paces long, four paces
Wide; an open flush-pit-latrine rested
In each courtyard to allow those most
'Trusted' henchpersons (including those
Brothers, sisters, nephews, nieces etc
And uncles of the official mistresses)
To exercise their bowels after the coup
(A wobbly shower was bracketed nearby).
You saw that tough wiregauze knocked
Over the courtyard to stop stray clods
From the guards' kids outside falling
In and hurting the notorious dissidents
And rebels as they pined for the sun
In the yard. They called that adjunct
To Mikuyu Prison (where dangerous rebels
Like you first arrive) the New Building
Clearly, as distraction from the horror
Imbedded in that infamous Dzeleka Prison
Where these squalid prison conditions
Were born, after our dear cabinet-crisis.

III

That annexe writ large they'd christened
Mikuyu Prison where we circumcise you today;
And naming this prison after the noble
Biblical figs was flippant blasphemy to
Jesus who'd accused the figs of fruitless-
ness when he obviously saw it was out of
Season. But the Beast's remaining Party
Executives would have been gathered into
One of these eight large cells here divided
Into fourteen little cells, two paces by
One, named A-wing, where only grey-haired
Bambo Machipisa Munthali now clocks twenty-

four years (we call him Nelson Mandela
Of Malawi; you'll recognize him by his
Shaven head every Christmas in memory of
His mother and the Chambers Dictionary he's
Allowed beside his Bible). In A-wing then
The Monster's ministers would reconsider
Their allegiances after the bloodless coup.
And with the nation's doctors, teachers,
Diplomats, journalists, lawyers, pastors,
Farmers, all the other nameless bumblebees,
Some seven hundred and eighty-eight freaks
Once (who'd have been released upon take-
over) cramming the other seven large Mikuyu
Cells, the pact would've been clinched
Without fuss. But the Brute invoked his
Charms, the Chief of Special Branch and
The Secretary General of the Party crashed
Here, opening the gates of the New Building,
Mopping the wagtail shit of their creation!
The Chief eventually went bonkers and is
Quietly lodged at Zomba Central Prison
And the Secretary General opted to hang.
(They'd overlooked the cornerstone beacons
That attracted hundreds of wagtails outside,
Turning the wiregauze over the yard into
Overnight wagtail nests and shaping these
Nightmares future detainees will mop!)

IV

We won't bother you with cases of these
Sparrows in D4, talk to them to share
Their humour; but let not the years some
Swallows have clocked here horrify you
(Sixteen, eleven, seven, that's nothing),
Rebels have been released here after one
Day; did you hear how Dick Matenje, Aaron

Gadama, Twaibu Sangala and David Chiwanga
Got released after one night in the New
Building and how the Special Branch who
Came to set them free suspiciously refused
To put their signatures in Gatebook 23
(Which carefully disappeared afterwards)?

V

But there's more. Take the other wagtails
Of Mikuyu Prison; these that chatter in
Circles, showing off their fluffy wings
To you, singing all day – watch how their
Splendour presages your visitors if you
Are allowed any here; and do not scare
These inmates; for, when acute malaria
Or cholera (we don't split these here!)
Admits you to Central Prison Sick Bay,
These wagtails will follow to minister
To you, these are the only priests allowed
Here and the dragon-flies, hundreds of moths
In golden robes, the geese floating over
Us and more, bringing messages of cheer,
Foretelling releases to come. Don't laugh,
When the day locks up, these wagtails
Twitter another tale; you won't laugh
When this courtyard wiregauze fills with
Thousands of wagtails that sleep standing
On one leg, head under wings, snoring
About today, fabricating their stinking
Shit on the courtyard below for us to mop
Tomorrow; and everyday you must mop this
Courtyard to survive the stench; D4 has
Even devised wagtail shit-mopping rosters,
The best in the land, definitely by far
Better than your skipping without ropes
At New Building! D4 is divided into dawn

Shifts too, ensuring your choicest weevil-
infected red kidney beans from these pots;
Happily, D4'll spare you the dawn kitchen
Shifts, though the vampires of New Building,
Those ticks in the cracks of cement floors
Still testify here; the fleas in the pores
Of your desert skin, those hyenas yapping
Worse than leprous midnight dogs, those
Scorpions whose sting sings like brain
Tumour, the swarming mosquitoes and bats;
What, who won't you find here, welcome
To these chattering wagtails of Mikuyu!

Scrubbing the Furious Walls of Mikuyu

Is this where they dump those rebels,
these haggard cells stinking of bucket
shit and vomit and the acrid urine of
yesteryears? Who would have thought I
would be gazing at these dusty, cobweb
ceilings of Mikuyu Prison, scrubbing
briny walls and riddling out impetuous
scratches of another dung-beetle locked
up before me here? Violent human palms
wounded these blood-bloated mosquitoes
and bugs (to survive), leaving these vicious
red marks. Monstrous flying cockroaches
crashed here. Up there the cobwebs trapped
dead bumblebees. Where did black wasps
get clay to build nests in this corner?

But here, scratches, insolent scratches!
I have marvelled at the rock paintings
of Mphunzi Hills once but these grooves
and notches on the walls of Mikuyu Prison,
how furious, what barbarous squiggles!
How long did this anger languish without
charge without trial without visit here and
what justice committed? This is the moment
we dreaded; when we'd all descend into
the pit, alone; without a wife or a child
without mother; without paper or pencil
without a story (just three Bibles for
ninety men) without charge without trial.
This is the moment I never needed to see.

Shall I scrub these brave squiggles out
of human memory then or should I perhaps
superimpose my own, less caustic; dare I
overwrite this precious scrawl? Who'd
have known I'd find another prey without
charge without trial (without bitterness)
in these otherwise blank walls of Mikuyu
Prison? No, I will throw my water and mop
elsewhere. We have liquidated too many
brave names out of the nation's memory;
I will not rub out another nor inscribe
my own, more ignoble, to consummate this
moment of truth I have always feared!

The Famished Stubborn Ravens of Mikuyu

These could not be Noah's ravens, these crows
of Mikuyu Prison groaning on our roof-tops each
day; wherever they wandered after their bungled
pilgrimages in the aftermath of those timeless
floods, Noah's ravens could not have landed
here (they never returned to their master's ark).
These could not be Elijah's ravens either; for
however stubbornly this nation might challenge
Lord Almighty's frogs, these devouring locusts,
the endless droughts and plagues, today there's
no prophet God so loves as to want to rescue
(with the bread and meat from messenger ravens!).

These can only be from that heathen stock of
famished crows and carrion vultures sent here
to peck at our insomnia and agony-blood-eyes
and to club the peace of this desert cell with
their tough knocking beaks. And why don't they
choose some other place and some other time?
Why must these crows happen at Mikuyu Prison,
always at dawn, hammering at the corrugated
iron of this cell, drilling at the marrow of our
fragile bones and picking at the fishbones
thieved from the dustbins we ditched outside?

To the Unknown Dutch Postcard-Sender (1988)

I

Your *Groeten uit Holland* postcard, with
Five pictures, dear unknown fighter for
My freedom, should not have arrived here
Really; first, your shameless address:
There are too many villages 'NEAR ZOMBA,
MALAWI', for anything to even stray into
Mikuyu Prison; then, I hear, with those
Bags upon bags of protest letters, papers,
Books, literary magazines, postcards,
Telexes, faxes and what not, received at
Central Sorting Office Limbe Post Office
Everyday, later dispatched to my Headmaster
And his henchpersons and the Special
Branch and their informers to burn, file
Or merely sneer at and drop in dustbins;
Your postcard had no business reaching
Mikuyu Prison. And how did you guess I
Would eventually sign my Detention Order
(No. 264), October 21, and I desperately
Desired some other solidarity signature
To stand by (to give me courage and cheer)
However Dutch, however enigmatic, stamped
Roosendaal, posted Den Haag 23 Oktober
1988, to buttress this shattered spirit
And these mottled bare feet squelching
On this sodden life-sucking rough cement
Of Mikuyu Prison ground? But many thanks,
Many thanks on behalf of these D4s too!

II

You send me those Dutch tourist colours
I'd probably have spurned outside; but
In these soggy red-brick and cracking
Cement walls, a sun-burned Dutch *clogger*
In black cap, blue shirt, orange apron,
Chocolate trousers and brown wooden shoes
Selling white, red, and yellow clogs,
Beside a basketful of more white clogs
Is spectacle too tantalizing for these
Badly holed Levi's shoes and blistered
Feet! You offer me Dutch menfolk in
White trousers and white shirts and red,
Blue, and yellow hats declaring heaps
On heaps of Edam cheeses on oval-shaped
Pine trays buoyantly shaming our ghoulish
Goulash of gangrenous cow bones mashed
In rabid weevil-ridden red kidney beans!
You proffer Dutch bell-shaped houses beside
Fruit trees, a family strolling along
The avenue; this concrete church with
Arches and Corinthian columns probably
Beat the bombs; a Dutch mother and daughter
In white folk-hats and black and white
Pretty frocks sitting on trimmed green
Lawn, offer each other red tulips beside
A colony of yellow tulips; and I present
You these malaria infested and graffiti
Bespattered walls, without doctors, priests
And twelve months of barred visits from
Wife, daughters, son, relatives, friends!

III

But however these colours slipped through
The sorters, your *Groeten uit Holland*,
My dear, has sent waves of hope and reason
To hang-on to the fetid walls of these
Cold cells; today the midnight centipedes
Shriller than howling hyenas will dissolve;
We will not feel those rats nibbling at
The rotting corns of our toes; and that
Midnight piss from those blotched lizards
Won't stink; and if that scorpion stings
Again tonight, the stampede in D4 will jump
In jubilation of our *Groeten uit Holland*.

Mikuyu Prison Visit of Head of Detainees

At the office gate, the guard-commander
Stands at attention. 'Special Branch!' he
Whispers, his forefinger crossing his lips.

The wooden bench creaks to my nerves.
I recognize the thin man. He ransacked
My life last September, scattering books,

Papers, records; violently quarrelling
With mother and my six-year, anger-choking
Son, 'You got cheek to bind my dad thus!'

He returned here in October 'for security
Reasons' to get me to sign my Detention
Order; 'Sign here, beside His Excellency

Life President's own signature' (so visibly
Photocopied from the Malawi Congress Party
Card of 1960, perhaps for security reasons!).

The other man, double chinned, cheeks
Still puffed from yesterday's Christmas
Carlsbergs, has hands stinking of tomato-

boiled dried fish he had for Christmas.
Why do they choose unlikely salamanders
To taunt us with death, further charges

Or freedom? Why don't they just minister
To their migraines at home after the hectic
Christmas chase of their vaporous rebels?

'You've been summoned to meet the Head of
Detainees.' I wonder what I'd be doing on
Boxing Day. 'I have been sent by Inspector

General to find out what your problems are.'
Silence. 'Have you got any problems then?'
Silence. Have I got problems? I can't talk

About the weevils in my food; I can't ask
For the medical doctor, not allowed here;
I can't want the priest, banned; I can't

Say, 'Even police magazines don't reach
Here!' I can't this; can't that; can't –
'Yes, as a matter of fact, I do have two

Problems; one, I don't understand why
My wife and children are not allowed to
See me here; two, I want to apologize

But since I was neither charged nor tried,
How does one go about apologizing?' Their
Eyes meet, gleaming. Head barks for paper

And pen. Guard-commander quickly brings
Five-hundred ream of A4 paper and biro.
'If you put down here those complaints,

I'll take your letter to the Inspector
General personally myself, today. Take
Your time; we are here for you; we can

Wait for three hours, up to about one?'
The smell of fresh A4 paper overpowers.
The biro feels strange on fingers after

Fourteen months. I remember the tests I
Took in the dusty classrooms of Kadango.
After forty minutes and several drafts,

Humiliation resolves: you must apologize
About something, for somebody's sake, man!
Right: Dear Right Honourable Inspector

General, I do apologize, from the bottom
Of my heart, to His Excellency the Life
President, his government, his university

Authorities 'for any embarrassment caused
Or to be caused by my detention!' Also,
As I left behind a very sick mother, wife,

Three asthma children, I do sincerely hope
Your Honourable Office can kindly get my
Case reconsidered. Your obedient servant . . .

The Head folds the two pages into his
Jacket pocket, assuring me the letter
Has arrived. The junior man touches me

Goodbye. The Head kindly offers to throw
My shredded drafts in the dustbins of his
Police officers' mess at home. I oblige.

The Tale of a Dzeleka Prison Hard-Core Hero

(For Madhala)

'The landrover stops one hundred yards from
Dzeleka Prison gate; the two rows of those

Notorious guards you have heard about blur,
Their clubs or truncheons raised high to kill.

They unlock your leg-irons whose clump now
Numbs; they take off your handcuffs in blood.

Your garments are like Jesus's, except that
Like the other thief you have indeed robbed,

Many times, and several even armed. It was
The Congress Party wallet you threw in Shire

River that has brought you to Dzeleka Prison;
You could not stop pinching just to please

The name they gave this prison; how could
You stop picking the Congress Party mango?

It's the only fruit you pick without guilt:
They forced it off the poor, you off them,

Wash out! But you must run very fast between
Those rows to get to the end of that human

Tunnel alive. I remember only the sudden
Naked shiver; the rest you can guess. Yet

Imagine the whole Presidential tour to Taiwan
To import for us the one and only hard-core!

(Indeed, fancy all those Western freedoms he
Watched, wasted on such dull despot desires –

The streets of Taiwan are so tidy; no thieves,
No beggars; that's a nation for you! he boasts.)

God, I miss those juicy avocado pears behind
The Congress Party fence in Kabula Old Museum!

And awaiting to hang must be dead end here; I
Mean, there's no second chance in Mikuyu Prison,

Is there? And that stupid traditional court
Judge, Moses, did he also ask you fellows to

Produce in court the person you'd sorted and
When you could not, did the devil also squeal:

Go and wait for your victim at Mikuyu Prison?
What village justice brought you to doom here?"

The Trip of Chief Commissioner of Prisons (1990)

Having known how these barbed wires
Throttle, it's surprising that our
Chief Commissioner of Prisons should
Have so thoughtlessly invented his
Own dreams to run our cockroach lives
On. Who does not know the official
Gweru Prison dreams this nation is
Supposed to totter on; who does not
Know he was neither imprisoned himself
Nor does he want to hear of those who
Were (in colonial times or these)?
Even these stinking bats of Mikuyu
Prison know everything (or nothing);
Yet how could Chief Commissioner
Take so lightly His Excellency's Gweru
Prison dreams that rule our gecko lives?
How did his precious skill, to build
An additional prison in each district,
Crowning his ambition of another state
That boasts more prisons than hospitals,
How did his scheme hatched for the nation
In the image of his Nyau Mask Dances,
Finally slip? (Indeed, why not, why
Not build more prisons when dissidents
Forever lurk around these tenacious
Borders, confusing 'His Excellency Life
Monocracy's' Peace & Calm, Law & Order?)

But having so faithfully built those
Prisons and prison-farms in each and
Every district, having spoofed those
Village Headmen, first could they offer
Their cows, goats, ducks, then their

Fertile land nicely turned into estates
In gratitude for Monocracy's contribution
To the development of 'the warm heart
Of Africa'; having so abundantly re-
distributed the prisons' free labour,
The bags upon bags of fertilizer, among
The Village Headmen and the Chief's
Relatives; having swindled bags upon
Prison bags of beans, maize, cabbage,
Rice to make the prisons self-sufficient
(Though alas, the prisoners still insist
On their marasmus estates!); why did
Our Chief Commissioner of Prisons have
To liberally fabricate his prison-farms
With *Malawi gold* – those darling Nkhota-
Kota tulips these prisons won't smoke?
What happened to all those connections,
How could his humour so badly trip?

The Delight of Aerial Signs of Release

(For Pat, David, Lan, Angus & Co)

I

'And there, rebels will rot, rot, rot!'

II

Today, remembering the tyrant's boast,
I began to seek aerial signs of release
To take the brag on; then your thoughts
Warm, the bulletins, your precious verse
Burrowed in, rocking our walls of despair
And the jangling locks and keys; the boots
Today tensed to your honorary membership
Cards of International PEN (English
Centre and American Center), Rotterdam
Poetry International award, Fund for
Free Expression New York, distinguished
Writers' demonstrations at 33 Grosvenor
St, London, Glasgow, Edinburgh, Toronto
And other adoptions: the Poetry Society
And Irina Trust, the BBC, Radio Deutsche
Vella, Radio Netherlands International,
Amnesty International, Africa Watch etc . . .
What spirit uplift, what hope repaired!
What parallels, what crushing solidarity!

III

Yet you say David Constantine's fine
Birthday lines to Irina Ratushinskaya
Encapsulate the frustration you feel

On your tough campaign for our release?
Of course, we have the verse in common
Also sweet exiles and gentle bravados
Against despots, so courage brethren;
You have combed enough of the beast's
Fleas to dispel the stench of our mire:
The head of detainees peeped in recently;
Mrs Thatcher was here, also the Pope;
The Moderator of Church of Scotland
Followed the Archbishop of Canterbury;
Even SADCC university ambassadors have
Been; do you realize the State House
Reply to your Edinburgh University
Appeal was forged? Your noble part is
Done; let the Gods take the arena now!

IV

Exampli gratia, only last Friday
Thousands of dragon-flies swarmed
Over our prison yard like hungry
Locusts brooding over tender green
Shoots; we held tight the memories
That keep these sagging souls alive
As nyapala Disi dispersed our fears:
This spectacle you see above has
Been here once in the fourteen years
Of my trial; two hundred political
Prisoners walked out of these gates
Free, reducing the seven hundred
And eighty-eight stinking breaths
That crammed these dark chambers!
He pointed to Allah above in glee.

V

And today, as the damp Mikuyu walls
Begin to lichen, hundreds of moths
(Ostentatiously spotted in gold on
Black, green on pink, white on purple,
What not) land on this rusting wire-
gauze; but before I feel my pulse,
Disi brings me more from the walls
To fondle, he says; since I defend
Even the rats that nibble at those
Rare home-brought avocados or these
Lethal mosquitoes, why don't I count
The spots of these moths to see how
Allah kindly brightens our abattoirs?
And I surprise myself how quickly I
Chorus Disi's: *This spectacle too*
Has happened once in this fourteen
Years ordeal here and more political
Prisoners will soon march past these
Stubborn gates of Mikuyu . . . Christ,
These airy signs are thrill to seek!

THE RELEASE AND OTHER
CURIOUS SIGHTS

The Release: Who Are You, Imbongi?*

(We've detained more distinguished people than you in this country, but we've never had the same amount of trouble as we've had over your case. WHO ARE YOU?)

When the lion wrung the gazelle
Under his smoking armpits, when
The foaming rhinoceros pierced his
Sharp horn or the leopard pounced;

Did you ask, *imbongi*, who are you?
(Even this underwear feels rough after
Three years, seven months, sixteen
Days and tweed jacket fungus-stinks,

Itching like ancient goat-skins);
Once upon a prison, perhaps after
Concourse of Life President and his
Inspector General, some handcuffed

Scarecrow jumped on landrover rack
To be interviewed fifty miles away;
Avidly he soaked up the sudden light,
Curious about the dwarfed maizescape,

And the dry mango trees. And despite
Blighted tomatoes and rotten bananas,
Famous Mbulumbuzi Market fuelled his
Landrover with boiled groundnuts; but

Mikuyu's last word stifled his hope
For appetite, 'If this is your release,
Then best wishes, remember you have
Left behind fellow inmates; if further

Charges, Mikuyu will gladly welcome
You back; if otherwise *accidentalized*
Our Gatebook signatures will testify.'
(Don't I recall Special Branch nervous

Signatures in Mikuyu Gatebook 23, 1983
That witnessed Gadama & Co's 'release'?)
Why didn't anybody warn me they might ask
Who I was on my release? But try these

Afterjokes for answer: he's mere *maccah*,
Just another burr that'll tenaciously
Stick to your cloth when you walk these
Wearing grass-roots; he's the persistent

Brown ant that crept into the elephant's
Ear, scratching, scratching, scratching,
Until elephant destroyed himself; watch
Your trousers; he won't shrug off your

Soggy sock that easy; so don't ask whence
Imbongi comes! On this tenth day of May
In this 1991st year of Our Lord, in order
To celebrate his official birthday – *His*

Excellency the Life President is pleased
To release you, accept our congratulations!

* *Imbongi*: praise poet

72

Tethered Border Fugitives upon Release

(For Mercy & the children, 1991)

Upon release, when I was mad about those
hasty grass-thatched mudhuts mushroomed

Below the grey boulders of Kirk Range
and the women & children who emerged

From them with the stench of civil wars
& harrowing tales (how senseless war-

psychopaths phanga-skewered their sons'
balls before their very eyes!); it was

Not their mudscape (which reminded me
of my childhood initiation grass-huts

& the dawn, ice-cold water into the ears
poured by the harsh words of the village

Chaperons I'd escaped); it was the horror
of those persistent mirrors I feared.

And when you wondered at those handshakes
of American refined vegetable oils, those

Italian *carne bovina in brodo* you bought
from the dear captives besides the tarred

Highway & brought into the shit-reeking
cells of Mikuyu Prison 'to mend another

Dislodged mortal flinching in the muck
of weevil-beans & the weeping bonfires

Of freckled geckos', you mocked; when you
intensely succoured those border fugitives,

Did you expect to see this other ghost
so tethered upon release?

These Straggling Mudhuts of Kirk Range

(For Brown & George, 1991)

Four years ago a battered initiate
Staggered out of those grass-huts
From a contraption of stunted weed,

Torn cartons and witch-oil-black
Cardboards held together by split
Bamboo and cords of bark; and trapped

In the heat between these hostile
Boulders and the misty valleys of
Villa Ulongue, she nervously peered

Into the tarmac of our makeshift
Borders, her wind-blown babe suckling
The bitter sweat of her dry breasts,

Her teeth (tartarred by wild fruit
On flight) exposing embittered memories
Of yet another home charred, goats,

Ducks and chicks scattered by shrapnel
From the enemy: her own people. But
Today, from these sprawling mud-shacks

Permanently huddled below Kirk Range
And sometimes threatening to leap like
Sand-frogs in the rain but beaten back

Squatting like grey turtles stuck
Between Inkosi Gomani's dwindling grave
And the tarmac road; today, from this

Straggling shackscape a chaperon and
A boy defiantly declare their UNHCR
Wares beside the highway: tins of butter

From European Community mountains,
Paraffin glass lanterns from Mozambique
And gallons of American cooking oil

(Bartering for the much needed dry fish
The donors overlooked). Today, the mother
Even manages a bleak joke about her son's

Father who slunk back home to smuggle
What remained behind of his own but never
Came back! But watch this woman tomorrow.

After the Berlin Wall, watch the tramp
She mothers in this triangular struggle
For these crusty boulders. And she is

Not oblivious of the sand shifting under-
foot nor those multipartisms embarrassing
These starved implacable borders! Watch.

The Baobab Trees of Our New Dependence

(For NWS, London, 1991)

In your multiparty promises, I fear
For those buxom baobabs most of all.
I fear he will invent other viral
Gimmicks to scupper those blossoming
Baobabs of Nkope Hill. He was never
Fond of exotic trees, you see, nor
The children's riddles about them (God
Made me upside down, trunk without
Neck, fingers without palms, but food
And shelter, who am I?); he never felt
Close to such baobab riddles, let alone
The brightness of their ash-green hue.
You saw recently how melodies, mere
Melodies of one fish-eagle perched on
Baobab twigs, before swooping down for
Its *chambo*, how mere voices threatened
Him!

                             Others
Dread the leeches of Milimbo lagoon,
Across the lake, how they suck the thigh's
Blood as you catch little herrings on
Safety-pin hooks in dug-out canoes (and
You need fire to burn the stubborn buggers
Out!); but he has no quarrel with leeches,
Only the baobab trees, those lovely rows
Of baobabs punctuated by cactus (to keep
The elephants out). Will he allow more
Fish-eagles to sing on our baobabs then?
Won't he fudge another virus to smother
Those succulent baobabs of Nkope Hill?

Your Tears Still Burn at My Handcuffs (1991)

After that millet beer you brewed, mother
(In case Kadango Mission made something of
Another lake-son for the village to strut

About!); and after that fury with Special
Branch when I was brought home handcuffed –
'How dare you scatter this peaceful house?

What has my son done? Take me instead, you
Insensitive men!' you challenged their threat
To imprison you too as you did not '*stop*

Your gibberish!' – After that constant care
Mother, I expected you to show me the rites
Of homing in of this political prisoner,

Perhaps with ground herbal roots dug by
Your hand and hoe, poured in some clay pot
Of warm water for me to suffuse, perhaps

With your usual wry smile about the herbs
You wish your mother had told you about.
Today, as I invent my own cleansing rites

At this return of another fugitive, without
Even dead roots to lean on, promise to bless
These lit candles I place on your head and

Your feet, accept these bended knees, this
Lone prayer offered among these tall unknown
Graveyard trees, this strange requiem mustered

From the tattered Catholic Choir of Dembo
Village. You gave up too early, mother: two
More months, and I'd have told you the story

Of some Nchinji upstart who tamed a frog at
Mikuyu Prison, how he gave it liberty to invite
Fellow frogs to its wet niche, dearly feeding

Them insects and things; but how one day,
After demon bruises, his petulant inmate
Threw boiling water at the niche, killing

Frog and visitor. And I hoped you'd gather
Some tale for me too, one better than your
Grand-daughter's about how you told her she

Would not find you on her return from school
That day. But we understand, after so many
Pointless sighs about your son's expected

Release, after the village ridicule of your
Rebellious breasts and sure fatigue of your
Fragile bones, your own minders, then your

Fear for us when the release did finally come –
You'd propose yet another exile, without you –
We understand you had to go, to leave us space

To move. Though now, among the gentle friends
Of these Jorvik walls, I wonder why I still
Glare at your tears burning at my handcuffs.

Where Dissent Is Meat for Crocodiles

(A Martyrs' Day History, 3 March 1992)

Since the cyclone *domoina* first
Lashed out its tail on those *sanjika*
Brimful dug-outs, since the first
Revolt at the nation's conception,
This monster of state we openly hope
To tame, regardless, continues rest-
lessly to breed its plethora of
Baffling metaphors benumbing even
The children. But this beast is vile;
It has persistently blatantly wrung.
And squelched nimble necks of sparrows
And hanging them tight between sharp
Split bamboos for the universe to
Watch and mock, dangled them in the sun
Until the last drop of truth has
Fallen. This beast we seek to acquit
And confirm has poisoned the crown
Of the rhino's horn without tears
Or shame; the very falcon has failed
To perch on those mango branches for
Prey. What of the blood of protesting
Students and starving workers? What
Of cudgelling to death these helpless
Mortals bailing out women wearing
Trousers at *jando* (that circumcision
Right for boys)? Today, his dossier
Thickens with more, clotting, stodgy
Figures, some that still bloodily flow
Unabated. And you brethren in dissent
Are out of bounds, meat for crocodiles,

Mere cliché in our country's anthology
Of martyrs, perhaps even smudges on
The blank page of this nation and our
Tyrant's boast of crocodile images
Of power. But in a century crying out
For love, what rancorous metaphors!

Canadian Geese Flying Over Alison's House

(For Alison Gordon & Austin Clarke, July 1992)

When you wondered how the Toronto summer
Rains could debase your barbecue before
That collage of artists and human rights
Sages, reading at the Harbourfront and
Celebrating the identity of the African
Diaspora as you rescued your brazier,
Deftly separating the sizzling sausages
From glasses of sparkling 'Canadian' wine;

Do you remember my distracting you with
That splendour of Canadian geese flying
High above your house? I said, that chain
Of geese flying thus over Mikuyu Prison
From Lake Chilwa towards Zomba mountain
Ranges, gently criss-crossing, meant
Release of as many political prisoners
Within weeks (I counted eight flying over
Your house before Dany and I absconded
To Austin's post-midnight mature rum!).

But when I returned to these lovely York-
shire moors and peaceful Jorvik gates,
Did I have to wait for weeks to hear of
The last eight political prisoners I had
Left at Mikuyu Prison released (boasting
Nineteen, fourteen, ten, six . . . four years
Incarceration without trial or charge);
I presume you are not bothered by such

Superstitious links, but I must confess,
The lure of these liberation campaigns
Delayed my gratitude for your hospitality!

You Caught Me Slipping Off Your Shoulders Once

(For Tukula Sizala Sikweya, 1992)

Today, when I heard of your release from Mikuyu
Prison after your fourteen years ordeal (for

Merely being nephew to your exiled rebel uncle
Or for winking at Inspector General's concubine)

I recall the frog you tamed (whose plot now
Thickens) and how you meticulously separated

The insects and craftily extracted the maggots
From those rotten cabbages in the dustbin heaps

Of Mikuyu Prison. I remember how your sharp
Breaths triumphantly bellowed weevils off those

Lobules of red kidney beans soaked overnight,
To salvage a semblance of a meal for us after

Moving me from isolation cell. You defiantly
Deflated the tedium of our years, cheering our

Despair with your contentious tales: you had
Smoked through worse horrors of Central Region

Mask dances (the birth place of this nation's
Brutality!). 'What lies here?' you challenged;

'And while I am *nyapala* in D4, I will ensure
You outlive this poison ordeal!' you rasped

Venomously. Today, after outlasting all that,
And in the comfort of these Roman walls, I

Hear those commands you shouted at me, often
At midnight as the hyenas howled, when you knew

I was awake, 'Come and watch this moon!' you'd
Whisper. 'It goes past that gap once a month!'

Sometimes at noon, 'Climb my shoulders, view
Those trees blossoming outside, you will be

Blinded gazing at these sick walls; climb these
Shoulders man, that beautiful woman with three

Children sitting under those acacias outside
(And brought by the priest in green car) could

Be yours; climb, damn it!' you would bark as
My nervous feet leapt on to your lion shoulders.

I remember suspending tenaciously from the narrow
Window-sill and peeping outside in disbelief:

The green acacias dancing to Lake Chilwa breeze,
The chickens pecking under the guard's granary,

The jacaranda trees purpling in the distance,
The deep red flamboyant flowers, until my heart

Started, my feet began to sweat on your shoulders –
'My God, my wife and children! After twenty-two

Months! And Pat O'Malley in white collar!' You
Caught me mid-air, slipping off your shoulders

And mocking my timidity, watched the prison gates
Call my name. And today, from these peaceful

Jorvik gates, I gather, you and all those D4
Wagtails can now see the whole moon? Amnesty!

The Souvenir Shards of My Berlin Wall

(For Philip Spender & Peter Ripken, July 1992)

I

After our grave dialogues in Potsdam's Eduard-
Claudius-Club (about the things that fall
Apart or perceptions of our misconceptions)
Between writers of what was Eastern Europe
And writers of what still is Africa (diaspora
and all – the thought often mind boggles!);
After warm reunions with long lost friends
And artists some unknown but long admired,
After humbling presentations of signatures
In my book of poems and letters by writers
And linguists (from London, Edinburgh, Glasgow,
Kampala, Rotterdam, Dar., Vienna, Hamburg, Paris,
New York, Harare, Ibadan, Brussels, Kinshasa,
Berlin, Gaborone, Toronto, Soweto, Ife . . .);
After solidarity dockets of the struggle
(Distinguished demonstrations, festivals,
Awards, readings, verse, T-shirts, what not!)
For my liberation by mortals and mentors
Who adopted this prisoner of conscience;
Fear for this Mondialism now overwhelms!

II

Tobias Bange rightly questions the wisdom
Of my tears at this gathering and suggests
Instead, perhaps characteristically, a TV
Interview within the walls of the Staats-
Sicherheit Ein Haus in Potsdam (that State
Security house in Potsdam that innocently

Mingled with trees, shops, offices and refused
To be named prison, for security reasons!)
To offer me the rare chance to see the arch
Brutality of German prisons once in the light
Of my Mikuyu Prison (the ironies never end!).
I accept and re-examine yard-and-cell whose
Sick dimensions are now peculiar classrooms!
Tobias Bange tempts with the shattered Berlin
Wall and Brandenburger Gate to walk through
(However late in the day for me). He takes
Shots and buys me shards of the Berlin Wall
In plastic souvenirs sold by ex-Communist
Soldiers. I brood over the new walls European
Verse is bound to invent and what strategies
Capitalism will adopt to survive or repair
Centuries of totalitarian onslaught! Pause.

III

We stop on Niederkirchner St between two
Walls where metres of the original Berlin
Wall still stand tattooed in huge indelible
Graffiti – TACHELES! and fenced in tough wire-
gauze for future generations and me, flanked
By Gropius Museum on the left and another
Mock Berlin wall decked in colourful graffiti
On the right flanked by new scaffoldings
Of the ancient Prussian Parliament building.
Between these two walls (where Gestapos
On shifts jumped off running trucks once
To shoot climbers to freedom), there's drama:
A woman pulls out a hammer from her hand-
bag and begins frantically knocking down
The fake wall to bemused family-tourists
(Who won't tell clods of the true Berlin
Wall from crumbs of the fake Berlin Wall?);
Within minutes those once much dreaded

Polizei are on the scene; but this can
Only be another minor misperception best
Resolved with bows and smiles all round –
These fragile times of transition to sanity;
Tobias Bange blames it on the Berlin heat:
'Soon we'll be eating our own bananas!'

IV

It's now that I recall your office Wilfried
Ruprecht; I hear you defying the sun-burnt
Gardens of our cardboard Capital Hill (where
Marauding hyenas prowl within stubborn walls).
I remember how you gleefully recounted
The paradoxes of your Berlin Wall which
Miraculously crumbled while I was chained
And how nobly you took the indignity you
Suffered for our redemption at the hands of
Our stony ghosts. I beamed, imbibing Nelson
Mandela's release in disbelief in contra-
distinction to my own, mean and weeks old,
Pondering your multipartisms, human rights,
Good governance etc, fearing the traumas
These would open up amongst our impervious
Ravens and the stench of their dungeon
Bats. You thought I was too civil with
My summation of your unique face in this
Curious strife for Africa's new dependence
For I saw the diffuse shapes future brushes
Would paint to your memory and was jealous;
But I warned only about our slipping grass-
roots and the impending bloodbaths to be
Invented by our turgid cockroaches; you
Sincerely hoped the wounds wouldn't happen.

V

But today, as Tobias Bange points to more
Scaffoldings of apartments in Potsdam
And Berlin (where Politburo Executives
Still live in fear of their own images),
War-cries of home rebound; I see distant
Kitchen Revolts of students and workers
At Chirunga Estate and Matenje Village
Where rosaries are flying for new banners
Of familiar perceptions of our deceptions.
Thirty-three years ago Ndirande was locked
In the Clocktower Riots that liberated us
From British claws; now after the Bishops'
Pastoral Letter, Ndirande still spills
The blood of Independence not achieved!
Tomorrow, they'll scatter Ndirande, I fear,
To punish those riotous township rosaries
(And the world will probably turn away
Tangled in the exigencies of Sarajevo) –
I decipher the shards of my Berlin Wall.

For Madame Potiphar's Wasteaways

(To the memory of Sylvester Phiri, Alick Kadango and Frackson Zgambo who died recently in Mikuyu Prison, Malawi)

The tale of your sudden deaths invokes
Weird belly-aches. I did not know you as
Protesting rebels who might meet their
End tortured under the pretext of cerebral
Malaria. How could those dreams of motels
You madly designed and re-designed (with
Our stolen chloroquine tablets) all over
The coarse cement floors of Mikuyu, how
Could that generous humour have gone to
Waste so? Today, the blue jokes you trusted
Me with (on the origins of your ordeal)
Flash past: yours was the folly of willing
Fugitives netted in Madame Potiphar's soap
Operas, you said; and however dearly Madame
Potiphar desired to bid in your private
Businesses, you were neither Josephs lodged
Permanently with Yahweh nor did you intend
To govern Egypt's precious gold: yours was
The dull crime of staunch bodyguard loyalty.

So Madame Potiphar need not have bothered
To cast her eyes on your tunics, imputing
Fantasies she had already fulfilled. And
Why did she have to chuck you into dungeons
When she knew you had no power to interpret
Pharaoh's dreams, to deliver yourselves? But
Perhaps you were too naive, dear brothers;
You know how our vultures devour their young

Boasting about the shame they've never had;
How did you let them invent malaria for you?
Whatever, though I made no pledges, today
I feel guilty; they should have granted you
Full view of those stars we fought over on
D1 door-window; they should have freed you
Like all those inmates we left behind now
Freed and actively liberating their Mikuyu
Dreams from the claws of our stubborn vultures!

In Memoriam (For Orton Chirwa, 20 October 1992)

I

'Did you ever meet him in prison? How
Was he? We hear he's in leg-irons and
Chains for having attempted to smuggle
Out a letter?' Orton Chirwa, it's months
Now since your anxious friends pestered
Me about your health, shuffling those
Letters you wrote them in the struggle
For liberation of Nyasaland from British
Rule. We admired the tone you chose to
Beat the subtle understatements of Colonial
Office and wondered how that compatriot
You'd offered the colours of the Malawi
Congress Party you'd founded, could have
Eventually chained you and your wife for
Life? Where could we have gone wrong?
(Even the Yorkshire dales' crocuses within
The Roman walls of this ancient city blushed
At our approaching English summer haze.)
Orton Chirwa, four years ago, I entered
At midnight, that single cell of the New
Building Wing of Mikuyu Prison they dumped
You once. The walls spoke loudly your
Fanatics' tattoos *O.C., Q.C. was here, O.K.?*
And though you had moved when I arrived,
The legend of the foya-gowns you stitched
Together to make a mimicry of bedsheets,
To supplement your Chiperoni blanket rags
(Which probably wrung your neck today),
Your lore continued to urge us to combat
The stench of Mikuyu bats without bitterness.

II

But when they consigned you to those walls
Of Zomba we secretly feared for your brittle
Constitution. How were those rheumatic
Bones going to cope in another lonelier
And darker cell of Zomba Central Prison
Beside the executioner's tools? How'd
You get bulletins to bench your humour
On, and at what price, what leg-irons,
What handcuffs, what numbing chill of
Buckets of cold water on your naked body
For three days without food or water – what
Pneumonia we loathed! And today, I hear
They have frozen your fighting spirit
In the cramped mortuary of Zomba General
Hospital; will nobody mourn the rebel?
Will your dear wife (who probably took
Days to hear of your death) be allowed
To your burial? What of those children
With whom you shed tears in prayer for
Our country's Independence, will they
Be allowed to travel to mourn their dad?
Will that Livingstonia Presbyterian Choir
Sing your favourite psalm twenty-three?
And will they bury you among your own
Or in that cemetery near St Mary's where
They bury nameless, nondescript people?
(But whatever, peace; peace, for tomorrow,
From the chaos of our democratic fronts,
A monolith will tower to your memory and
The memory of those heroes and heroines
Our country may try to erase, peace!)

The Deluge after Our Gweru Prison Dreams

(After the 1992 Chirunga and Kabula riots by students and workers: a history of the nation, for David Rubadiri)

I

Today, the HM Prison Gweru dreams that
Fogged our vision once began to rupture

One by one: that pride of Capital Hill
Splintered in the heat of our endless

Droughts, the fallout muzzling the most
Civil of tenants; his luminous great

Lakeshore highway is crustaceous tarmac
In broken china, with yawning potholes

That crack landrover absorbers worse
Than those forest dirt roads long ago;

Even our quiet University students (having
Carefully balanced the shards of the beast's

Fantasies) only recently dared to sue
The Chairman of University Council for

Embezzling the truth and our University's
Head of Law for once defended justice!

II

After that happy debris of the Berlin Wall
And the Donor Community's 'good riddance?',

Which piqued goat won't feverishly nurse
His tics, stunned by the inexplicable

Directions of these anti-despot missiles?
And however often he might violently

Kick about the pact he made with the devil
Three decades ago when you abandoned his

Kraal, *I will dine with the devil himself
To centralize my Gweru dreams*, he revved;

Yet after our Nelson Mandela's release,
Even the devil's generosity must tire.

III

When battered hyenas fail to crack
Rotten bones in the dustbins of East

Versus West, the time has come for our
Youths to dance; and let them take

The arena; what phantom model would
Not shed her varnish and cower under

The strain of time and despot desires?
Those fatigued Ndirande varicose veins

Were bound to burst on to the streets
Of Kabula. And what scapegoats will

Be imagined, what rebels lurking on
Borders invented! But there was no

Masauko Chipembere, no Jomo Chikwakwa
This time to spur on these Ndirande

Grassroots beyond the fury of those
Rhinoceros horns of your Clocktower

Riots long ago; and let nobody load
It on Dunduzu or Yatuta Chisiza; there

Was no Silombera, no Kanada to publicly
Hang here; as for Aaron Gadama, Dick

Matenje, Twaibu Sangala, David Chiwanga . . .
They shamelessly accidentalized these.

IV

Yet the children are entitled to wonder
How we allowed it, how such Gweru prison

Vagaries, without true mystery without
Depth deluded us worse than our gods.

Indeed, who's never had prison dreams?
You must have locked up your own dreams

At HM Prison Khami, Bulawayo in 1959.
If wagtails at Mikuyu Prison only months

Ago dreamt their lizards and even I dreamt
Tearing up lions, hounds and leopards

Which in defeat served scones and tea
On bamboo trays to my released inmates,

If I fought gaseous reptiles, sometimes
Waking up the whole cell at midnight,

Shouting and heavily breathing – what,
Who's never had dreams in these daily

Prisons? But as the inmates at Mikuyu
Said afterwards, *Not even our nyapala's*

Deliria in D4 (and the bloody prefect's
Here without charge sixteen years) could

Dig anybody's pittance of pit latrine
With his Mikuyu dreams, let alone build

A nation! Whatever, the question still
Lingers: won't toxic mushrooms burgeon

Under those rotten logs of nightmares
That now threaten *après moi, le déluge?*

Glossary

bwezi The cheapest type of blanket.

chamba A kind of cannabis.

chambo An exceptionally delicious fish from Lake Malawi.

Chingwe's Hole A natural fault on Zomba plateau.

chitenje Cloth that women wrap around their waists.

mlombwa A tough tree.

Mphunzi Hills Known for their rock paintings (in Dedza District, central Malawi).

nsima Hard porridge made from maize, millet or rice flour.

nyapala A kind of 'prefect' in a cell.

sanjika A type of fish and the name of one of Dr Banda's palaces.

Shire Valley In southern Malawi.

tickies Threepenny pieces.

Zomba Once the capital town of Malawi, named after the plateau which dominates the town.